yukismart.com/b/6e4ee6

cat

кішка
kishka

dog

собака
sobaka

fish

риба
ryba

bird

пташка
ptashka

hen

курка
kurka

rooster

півень
piven

chick

курча
kurcha

egg

яйце
iaitse

cow

корова
korova

sheep

вівця
vivtsia

pig

свиня
svynia

goat

коза
koza

horse

кінь
kin

donkey

віслюк
visliuk

mouse

миша
mysha

rabbit

кролик
krolyk

turkey

індик
indyk

goose

гусак
husak

peacock

павич
pavych

duck

качка
kachka

duckling

каченя
kachenia

swan

лебідь
lebid

dragonfly

бабка
babka

fly

муха
mukha

ant

мураха
murakha

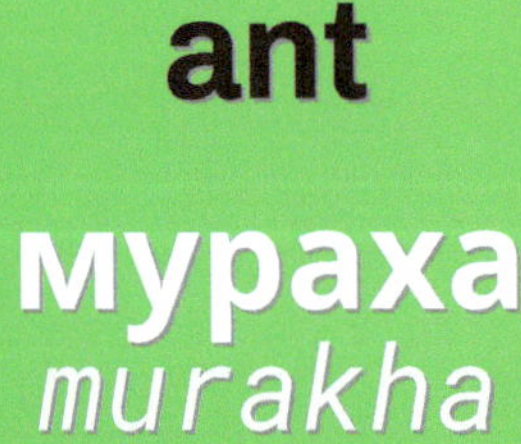

anteater

мурахоїд
murakhoid

ladybug

божа корівка
bozha korivka

earthworm

дощовий черв'як
doshchovyi cherv'iak

slug

слимак
slymak

caterpillar

гусениця
husenytsia

snail

равлик
ravlyk

butterfly

метелик
metelyk

grasshopper

коник
konyk

bee

бджола
bdzhola

honey

мед
med

spider

павук
pavuk

grass

трава
trava

beetle

жук
zhuk

mosquito

комар
komar

scorpion

скорпіон
skorpion

lizard

ящірка
iashchirka

turtle

черепаха
cherepakha

crab

краб
krab

shrimp

креветка
krevetka

lobster

омар
omar

whale

кит
kyt

shark

акула
akula

stingray

скат
skat

dolphin

дельфін
delfin

sea urchin

морський їжак

morskyi izhak

jellyfish

медуза

meduza

squid

кальмар

kalmar

starfish

морська зірка
morska zirka

seagull

чайка
chaika

sea

море
more

pelican

пелікан
pelikan

cormorant

баклан
baklan

shells

мушлі
mushli

sand

пісок
pisok

elephant

слон
slon

zebra

зебра
zebra

giraffe

жираф
zhyraf

snake

змія
zmiia

crocodile

крокодил
krokodyl

lion

лев
lev

tiger

тигр
tyhr

hippopotamus

бегемот
behemot

rhinoceros

носоріг
nosorih

cheetah

гепард
hepard

camel

верблюд
verbliud

antelope

антилопа
antylopa

flamingo

фламінго
flaminho

ostrich

страус
straus

stork

лелека
leleka

parrot

папуга
papuha

gorilla

горила
horyla

monkey

мавпа
mavpa

koala

коала
koala

panda

панда
panda

kangaroo

кенгуру
kenhuru

hedgehog

їжачок
izhachok

squirrel

білка
bilka

wolf

вовк
vovk

fox

лисиця
lysytsia

racoon

єнот
ienot

bear

ведмідь
vedmid

deer

олень
olen

eagle

орел
orel

bat

летюча миша

letiucha mysha

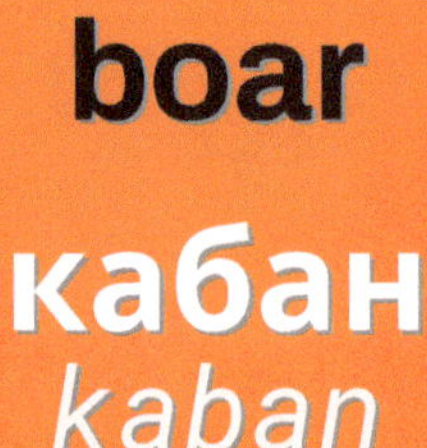

boar

кабан

kaban

crow

ворона

vorona

owl

сова

sova

woodpecker

дятел
diatel

polecat

тхір
tkhir

mole

кріт
krit

beaver

бобер
bober

polar bear

білий ведмідь

bilyi vedmid

snow

сніг

snih

penguin

пінгвін

pinhvin

snowy owl

біла сова

bila sova

forest

ліс
lis

mountain

гора
hora

narwhal

нарвал
narval

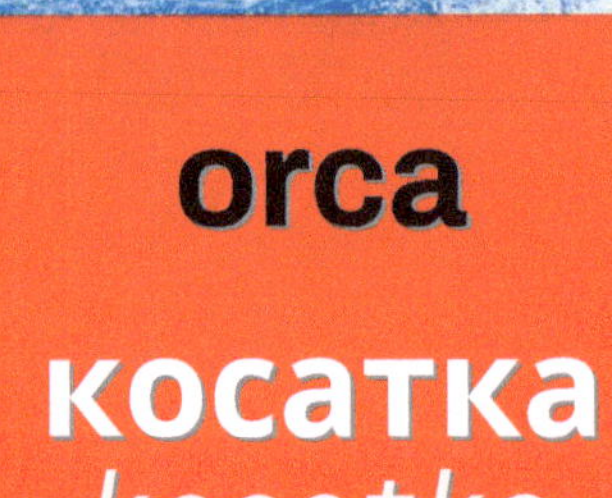

orca

косатка
kosatka

walrus

морж
morzh

seal

тюлень
tiulen